DATE			

Natural Disasters

Floods

by
Jean Allen

Consultant:
Roger A. Pielke, Jr.
National Center for Atmospheric Research

CAPSTONE
HIGH-INTEREST
BOOKS

an imprint of Capstone Press
Mankato, Minnesota

Capstone High-Interest Books are published by Capstone Press
151 Good Counsel Drive, P.O. Box 669, Mankato, Minnesota 56002
http://www.capstone-press.com

Library of Congress Cataloging-in-Publication Data
Allen, Jean.
    Floods/by Jean Allen.
    p. cm.—(Natural disasters)
    Includes bibliographical references (p. 45) and index.
    ISBN 0-7368-0900-7
    1. Floods—Juvenile literature. [1. Floods.] I. Title. II. Series.
GB1399 .A455 2002
551.48'9—dc21   00-013194

Summary: Describes how and why floods happen, the damage they cause, ways to
control them, and some of the most destructive floods of the past.

Editorial Credits
Gillia M. Olson, editor; Lois Wallentine, product planning editor;
    Timothy Halldin, cover designer and illustrator; Katy Kudela, photo researcher

Photo Credits
AP/Wide World Photos, 4
Archive Photos, 26, 28
Betty Crowell, 15, 38, 41
Bill Alkofor/St. Paul Pioneer Press, 30
Deutche Presse/Archive Photos, 16
Doug Sokell/TOM STACK & ASSOCIATES, 8
Eric R. Berndt/The Image Finders, 34
Inga Spence/Visuals Unlimited, 20
John Elk III, 24 (center)
Kay Shaw, 24 (bottom)
Martin G. Miller/Visuals Unlimited, 43
Photri-Microstock, 24 (top); Photri-Microstock/Brent Winebrenner, 10;
    Pete Petrisky, 18
Reuters/Juda Ngwenya/Archive Photos, 6
Richard Day/Daybreak Imagery, cover
Unicorn Stock Photos/Dennis MacDonald, 36
U.S.G.S., 22
U.S.G.S. Photo Library, Denver, Colorado, 32

1 2 3 4 5 6 07 06 05 04 03 02

Table of Contents ⟵

Chapter 1

Floods

In late February 2000, Cecelia Chirindza was caught in a flood from the Limpopo River in Mozambique. The water rose rapidly. Chirindza climbed to a platform in a tree to escape. The platform had been built quickly when the floods first started.

Chirindza was pregnant with her third child. The baby was due soon. Some of Chirindza's family members also were stranded in the tree. The muddy waters had been churning beneath them for four days. Chirindza's baby came sooner than she had expected. She was forced to have the baby on the platform.

Chirindza's mother-in-law helped her give birth to a healthy baby girl named Rosita.

Cecelia Chirindza had her daughter Rosita while stranded in a tree.

Many Mozambiquans were forced to evacuate during the 2000 floods.

Soon, a rescue helicopter spotted the group. A medical worker helped Chirindza and the baby to the helicopter. The rescue workers brought all the people stranded in the tree to dry land. Chirindza and the baby were rushed to a hospital.

Rosita made worldwide news as "the baby born in a tree." The event helped bring attention to the floods in Mozambique,

Zimbabwe, and neighboring countries. The floods lasted from February 9 to mid-March. Heavy rains occurred in the area for three weeks. The rain caused many area rivers to spill over their banks. The Limpopo River valley had some of the worst flooding.

The flooding in Mozambique and Zimbabwe left thousands of people stranded on rooftops or in waist-deep water. Parents hung onto trees with their children on their backs. In some cases, buildings collapsed under the weight of the people on the roof.

The floods caused a huge amount of damage. Floodwaters destroyed entire villages. Most crops and livestock were destroyed.

Many flood victims moved to relief camps. But the dirty floodwaters spread serious diseases such as cholera and malaria throughout the camps. Cholera causes stomach pains, diarrhea, vomiting, and sometimes death. Mosquitoes attracted by the water spread malaria. This disease causes fever and chills.

About 700 people died as a result of the floods. More than 2 million people were left

without homes or jobs. It was one of the worst floods in the region's history.

Floods

Floods are one of the most common natural disasters. A flood occurs when a body of water flows into areas that usually are dry. Floods take place throughout the world.

Floods can happen slowly. They can occur over days or weeks. More areas are flooded as high water works its way downstream.

Floods also can happen quickly. Flash floods occur within six hours of rainfall. Flash floods are very dangerous. The water moves rapidly and with great force. It can sometimes sweep away bridges, cars, and buildings. Most flooding deaths are due to flash floods.

People try to control and predict floods. People build structures to try to prevent floods. They also build computer models to try to predict floods. But floods continue to be a problem with no simple solution.

Floods can sweep away bridges.

Chapter 2

Why Floods Happen

Floods are a natural part of the water cycle. They actually benefit some areas by bringing rich soil for farming. Many weather and soil conditions can cause floods. People's actions also have contributed to flood problems.

Infiltration and Runoff

Heavy rains cause most floods. Rain can combine with other water sources to cause floods. Rain can flow in two directions when it hits the ground. Water can seep into the ground or flow along the surface.

Infiltration occurs when water seeps into the ground. The soil absorbs the water. This water soaks through the ground until it reaches the water table. This layer of earth remains

Floods can happen when water does not seep into the ground.

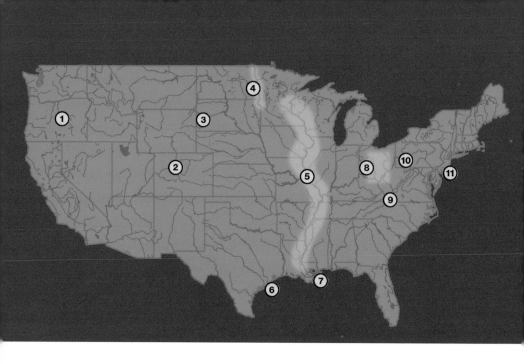

Deadly and Damaging U.S. Floods

Site and Year	Deaths	Damages*
1) Willow Creek in Oregon, 1903	225	unknown
2) Big Thompson Canyon, Colorado, 1976	144	$39 million
3) Rapid City, South Dakota, 1972	237	$160 million
4) Red River, North Dakota and Minnesota, 1997	8	$2 billion
5) Mississippi River Basin, 1993	48	$20 billion
6) Galveston, Texas, 1900, Hurricane	6,000	unknown
7) Gulf Coast (Mississippi and Louisiana), 1969	259	$14 billion
8) Ohio, statewide, 1913	467	$143 million
9) Buffalo Creek, West Virginia, 1972	125	$60 million
10) Johnstown Flood, Pennsylvania, 1889	2,200	unknown
11) Northeastern United States, 1938, Hurricane	494	$306 million

* Amounts are not adjusted for inflation.

soaked all or most of the time. The water in the water table is called groundwater. Groundwater is pumped into homes and businesses for people to use. Groundwater also flows into rivers and lakes.

Rain also can flow along the ground's surface. This water is called surface runoff. Surface runoff occurs when the ground cannot absorb any more water. It also occurs when the soil is too tightly packed. The dense soil does not absorb water quickly. Paved areas also cause surface runoff because these areas cannot absorb water. This water flows over land until it reaches a stream, river, lake, or ocean.

An area of land that drains into a body of water is called a watershed. Each watershed is part of a larger watershed. Water from a small area of land may drain into a small creek. That small creek might empty into a small river. The river may empty into an even larger river. This pattern forms a large river basin.

Flood-Producing Storms

Floods can occur when a watershed receives more water than it can drain. The rivers and streams cannot carry away or hold all the water. A single, slow-moving thunderstorm can dump large amounts of water in a short time.

A series of thunderstorms also can cause floods. This storm pattern is called training. Each storm is like a boxcar on a train track. A storm brings heavy rain to an area and moves on. One or more storms follow the first storm. The ground cannot absorb all the rain. The rain becomes surface runoff. Flooding then occurs.

Backbuilding is another storm pattern that produces floods. Backbuilding occurs when a storm's back edge continues to develop as the storm moves forward. The rain continues without a break for a long period of time.

Extreme flooding often is caused by heavy rainfall from tropical cyclones such as hurricanes. These storms form in the ocean's warmest areas. In July 1979, Hurricane Claudette caused one of the heaviest rainfalls ever recorded. In one day, this storm dumped 43 inches (109 centimeters) of rain on Alvin, Texas.

The storm surge of a hurricane can cause a coastal flood. During a storm surge, the wind

Arroyos and washes leave behind dry river beds.

piles up the ocean water and pushes it to shore. A storm surge can be more than 19 feet (5.8 meters) high. It can destroy everything in its path when it reaches land. The storm surge can affect an area that is hundreds of miles or kilometers wide.

Small amounts of rain can cause floods. This especially is true in the desert. Desert areas receive little rain. Flash flooding is a threat in desert areas of the southwestern United States. The soil in these areas becomes hard and dense.

Survivors from a town washed away by the Vaiont Dam failure visit the site.

When it does rain, the water does not soak into the ground. The water rushes across the ground's surface. It forms temporary rivers in channels called arroyos or washes.

Flash flooding especially is dangerous in canyons. Water runs down off the hard, steep canyon walls. It can quickly flood the bottom of the canyon. As little as .5 inch (1.3 centimeters) of rain could cause a deadly canyon flash flood.

Other Flood Causes

Floods also take place when dams break or cannot hold back the water. Huge amounts of water are released suddenly. Dam failures cause some of the world's deadliest floods. In 1963, a landslide in the Italian Alps mountain range pushed water over and around the Vaiont Dam. The resulting flash flood killed about 2,000 people. The disaster did not break the dam. But the dam failed to prevent a flood.

Ice jams also can cause floods. In northern climates, rivers freeze during winter. During spring, the rivers thaw. Huge chunks of ice break off. These chunks float downstream. They can pile up in a narrow part of the river or near a bridge or dam. The river can flood easily if the water cannot get past the ice jam.

Erosion contributes to floods. This process takes place when wind or water gradually wears away soil. Soil along riverbanks washes away quickly if there are no trees or large rocks to hold it in place. The soil can end up at the bottom of a riverbed. The riverbed becomes shallower. There is less room for extra water. A shallow riverbed is more likely to flood.

Chapter 3

The Power of Floods

People have been trying to predict and control floods for thousands of years. Today, scientists consider many factors when predicting floods. They develop estimates of the chances of future floods. They do this by studying past floods.

Flood Estimates

Scientists consider particular locations when they estimate the chances of a future flood. These estimates are based on how many floods occurred in a particular location in the past. But these estimates are not always correct. The future is not always like the past. Weather and climate do not stay the same.

Flood waters can be very powerful.

Scientists measure snow depth to estimate surface runoff.

Scientists may reconsider their estimates when a new flood occurs. This may help make future predictions more exact.

Predicting Floods

Scientists who try to predict floods look at many factors. Scientists first need to know the amount of groundwater entering a river or lake. This amount is called the baseflow. The baseflow changes often. It depends on the amount of water in the soil and underground. It also depends on recent rainfall amounts.

Scientists also need to know the amount of surface runoff. They pay close attention to rainfall in different areas. Soil density and the slope of the land will cause different amounts of runoff. Paved areas will have more runoff than non-paved areas.

Snow also contributes to runoff. In the spring, melting snow increases groundwater levels. The water table cannot absorb the extra water quickly enough. Scientists use snow depth, air temperature, and amount of sunshine to estimate how fast snow will melt.

Scientists also have powerful tools that help them to predict floods. These tools include Doppler radar. This system uses radio signals to create an image of rainfall on a monitor. The images also show where storms are most severe.

Automated gauges also are important. Scientists place them in or near rivers. The

Stream gauges can measure river depth and speed.

gauges can measure the amount of rainfall in an area. They also can measure a river's height and the water's speed.

The gauges send information automatically to a computer. Thousands of gauges are set up throughout the United States. Computer models generated by gauge information help scientists make flood predictions.

Watches and Warnings

The National Weather Service (NWS) issues flood watches and warnings. Watches are issued when scientists find out that conditions may cause a flood. Watches can cover entire states. The NWS usually issues watches 12 to 36 hours in advance.

The NWS issues warnings if floods or flash floods are occurring or very likely to occur. Warnings cover smaller areas such as single counties.

Flash floods still can be very difficult to predict. One problem is that flash floods often are part of another severe weather event. They may occur together with tornadoes or hurricanes. Different watches and warnings can be confusing. People might not have time to react.

Flood Control

People cannot prevent some factors that cause floods. But they can try to control floods. People can build structures that keep rivers from overflowing. They also can preserve wetlands near rivers and lakes.

Flood Control History

Huang He (Yellow River)

The Huang He flows across northern China. Erosion brings much silt into the river. These tiny soil particles often cause the river to change course or overflow. People have tried to control this river since 200 B.C. People dredged the river. They dug out the layers of silt from the riverbed.

But the high silt content continues to be a problem. Floods in 1887, 1931, and 1938 killed millions of people. This river has killed more people than any other river in the world. The Huang He often is called "China's Sorrow." The Huang He continues to be hard to control.

The Nile River

The Nile River in Egypt used to flood every year. The floodwaters left behind a thin layer of rich black soil. Farmers planted their crops in this rich soil. This farmland produced enough food to feed the entire population of Egypt. The annual flooding was called the "Gift of the Nile."

Crops now need to be planted year-round. The Aswan High Dam was built in 1970. It holds floodwaters in reservoirs. This water is slowly released during the dry season. But the naturally rich soil is gone. Farmers today must apply large amounts of fertilizer to the land.

The Mississippi River

The Mississippi River has the largest system of levees in the world. People built many of them after a severe 1927 flood. The levees made flooding less severe.

Since then more people have moved onto drained wetlands along the Mississippi River. Floods became more likely without the wetlands to absorb extra water. The levees were not enough to control the severe floods. In recent years, people have built hundreds of runoff canals and many dams. The system has prevented floods. But severe flooding still occurred in 1993.

Structures that control floods include levees, runoff canals, and reservoirs. A levee is a wall along the side of a river. Levees often are called dikes. They increase the height of the riverbank. Some levees are made of soil. Other levees are made of concrete. People sometimes pile sandbags to make temporary levees during an emergency.

Runoff canals also can control floods. People dig these narrow channels and connect them to rivers. The canals direct extra water away from a river during a potential flood. The water flows to a different area where it will not cause any harm.

Reservoirs can hold extra water during floods. These lakes build up behind dams or occur naturally. The dams have gates. People control the release of water through these gates. A steady amount of water then flows downstream.

Wetlands control floods naturally. Wetlands absorb extra water from floods. Some people build their homes or businesses on drained wetlands near rivers and lakes. These people are at risk for property damage or injury.

Chapter 4

Famous Floods

Throughout history, floods have caused a great deal of damage. U.S. floods have killed about 94 people each year during the last 10 years.

Johnstown Flood, 1889

In 1889, Johnstown, Pennsylvania, was a busy town of 30,000 people. Johnstown is located at the fork of the Little Conemaugh and Stony Creek Rivers. The South Fork Dam was located 14 miles (23 kilometers) up the Little Conemaugh River. The dam was made of packed dirt and rocks. It held Lake Conemaugh.

The dam was 450 feet (137 meters) higher in elevation than Johnstown. Townspeople knew that the dam was poorly maintained.

The Johnstown flood washed away much of the downtown area.

The flood even destroyed many brick buildings in Johnstown.

Every spring, they joked that the dam might not hold. In 1889, they were right.

It was a wet spring. On May 31, a steady rain fell that finally pushed the dam to its limits. At least two men on horseback rode through town. They shouted reports that the dam would fail. But many people did not listen to the reports. The dam broke shortly after 3:00 in the afternoon.

Soon after, 20 million tons (18 million metric tons) of water came tearing down the valley. The water reached a speed of 40 miles (64 kilometers) per hour.

There was no time to escape once the water reached Johnstown. Within 10 minutes, a large area of town had been washed away. Thousands of people were caught in the wave. Some were crushed by debris such as logs and parts of buildings. More than 2,200 people died that day. Many more were left homeless.

The Red River Flood, 1997

The winter of 1996–97 was fierce. North Dakota, South Dakota, and western Minnesota received record amounts of snowfall. The snow melted in the spring. The water from the melting snow flowed into the Red River of the North. The river could not hold all of the water.

Many towns along the river were flooded. Grand Forks, North Dakota, and East Grand Forks, Minnesota, received the most damage. These towns are separated by the Red River. At

the time, the combined population of the two towns was about 59,000. Nearly 90 percent of the population of those two towns was evacuated. Almost all of the buildings in East Grand Forks were severely damaged or destroyed. In Grand Forks, 75 percent of the homes were damaged.

Fire was another problem during the flood. Officials believe fires started when wires shorted out underwater. The shorts then caused nearby materials to burn. Many buildings in downtown Grand Forks burned completely. Firefighters had to work in waist-deep water to put out the flames.

The problems continued after the flood. For 13 days, the towns had no running water. It was another 10 days before tap water was safe to drink. More than 60,000 tons (54,000 metric tons) of debris were removed.

The cost of the damage in those two cities was $2 billion. But the evacuation efforts paid off. No one was killed in East Grand Forks or Grand Forks. Eight people did die in other areas during the flood.

Firefighters try to fight a fire that broke out in Grand Forks during the flood.

Big Thompson Canyon Flash Flood, 1976

On July 31, 1976, about 3,000 people were living or vacationing in Big Thompson Canyon in north central Colorado. A huge thunderstorm developed over the Big Thompson Canyon that evening. Storms in that area usually pass quickly. This storm continued to backbuild.

The storm dumped 10 inches (25 centimeters) of rain in six hours. The hard, steep walls of the canyon could not absorb the water. Rushing water pushed rocks and mud down the canyon walls. Some slid onto Highway 34. This landslide blocked the exit out of the canyon.

The water gathered at the head of the Big Thompson Canyon. It then surged down the Big Thompson River. In some places it formed a wall of water 30 feet (9.1 meters) high. The water reached speeds of 50 miles (80 kilometers) per hour. The river normally is just a few feet deep.

The flash flood killed 144 people. At least 88 people were injured. It was the worst natural disaster in Colorado's history.

This house almost was washed away by the Big Thompson Canyon flood.

Chapter 5

Surviving a Flood

Floods can happen without warning. People can take some simple measures to reduce their chances of injury and reduce property damage.

Staying Safe

People should first find out if they live in an area that is likely to flood. They should know if their property is above or below flood stage. Emergency management offices can provide this information. Insurance companies, the Red Cross, and other disaster relief organizations also can help.

Weather usually is the most important factor in floods. People should listen to the news during periods of heavy rains. Radio stations,

---

People can fill sandbags to help keep people and property safe.

▷ **Rescue workers may evacuate people during floods.**

TV stations, and some Internet web sites will broadcast flood watches and warnings.

People should prepare if a flood watch is announced. They should fill bathtubs, sinks, or jugs with water. The home's water supply may become polluted after a flood. People may want to pack a suitcase with clothes, medicines, and other necessary items. They must leave the area quickly if they are told to evacuate.

People should bring valuable items to higher floors. Patio furniture, bicycles, and other outdoor items should be moved inside. A battery-operated radio and spare batteries should be on hand in case the power goes out.

Flood Warnings

People should listen carefully to flood or flash flood warnings. Local officials will give instructions. People may be told to turn off the home's utilities. Utilities include gas, water, and electricity. Officials also may tell people to evacuate. If so, people should evacuate immediately. Flooded roads or traffic jams can strand people who wait.

People who are outside during a flood should move to high ground. They should stay away from rivers, creeks, and storm drains. They also should avoid wading through the water. Even shallow water can be dangerous if it is flowing quickly. People can be swept away by as little as 6 inches (15 centimeters) of water.

Cars are not safe places during floods. More than half of all people who die in floods are trapped in their vehicles. People should never try to drive over a flooded road. The water may be deeper than it appears. The car may stall in water. If this happens, they should immediately leave the vehicle. The water's force is strong and unpredictable. Just 2 feet (.6 meter) of water can carry away a car or lightweight truck.

After a Flood

A flood remains dangerous even after the water level goes down. Local authorities will keep people updated. Evacuated people should not return home until conditions are safe.

People should be careful when they do return to their homes. Flooded buildings may have structural damage. They could cave in.

Fire is another danger. People should not try to turn on their homes' utilities by themselves. They should wait for the utility workers to do so. Broken gas lines, flooded electrical circuits, and damaged appliances all can cause

Flood waters can sweep away and destroy cars.

fires. Blocked roads may prevent rescue units from responding if a fire occurs.

Disease

Disease is a threat from floods. Floodwaters may contain raw sewage, silt, oil, and spilled chemicals. These pollutants can get into the water supply. The Public Health Department will tell people when water is safe to drink. Bottled water or water collected before the flood should be used instead. Toilets should not be used until water utilities are working.

People can begin cleaning when the water supply is safe. Walls and floors should be cleaned with soap and water. They then should be cleaned with bleach to kill any germs. Food, mattresses, and stuffed furniture that came in contact with floodwaters should be thrown out. Mattresses and furniture cannot be properly cleaned to kill germs.

The Future of Floods

The number of floods varies over time. Some scientists believe that there will be more

Mattresses and furniture caught in a flood should be thrown out.

flooding in the future because of changes in global climate. Changes in global climate occur both naturally and as a result of human activities. Natural factors such as oceans, volcanic eruptions, and land use all affect climate. People can affect climate by cutting down forests, draining wetlands, and polluting land and water.

It is difficult to say how climate will affect flooding in the future. It is more certain that people add to the amount of damage caused by floods. They sometimes build homes and businesses in areas that are likely to flood. This practice increases the chances of property damage and loss of life.

Flood control structures such as dams and levees protect many populated areas. But these structures are not always possible or desirable to build. They cost large amounts of money. They hurt the environment by destroying animals' homes. They also can provide a false sense of safety. Floods can still happen even if dams and levees are in place.

Floods always will be a part of the water cycle. People will continue to struggle with floods and flood control in the future. But people who understand floods can help save lives and keep property safe.

Some people build houses in areas that are likely to flood.

Words To Know

debris (duh-BREE)—the remains of something that has been destroyed

evacuate (i-VAK-yoo-ate)—to leave an area during a time of danger

flood stage (FLUHD STAYJ)—the height at which flooding occurs for a particular body of water

gauge (GAYJ)—an instrument used for measurement; stream gauges can measure a river's depth and speed.

hurricane (HUR-uh-kane)—a large system of thunderstorms with strong winds that whirl around a calm center

reservoir (REZ-ur-vwar)—a natural or artificial structure that is a holding area for a large amount of water

utility (yoo-TIL-uh-tee)—a basic service provided to a community such as electricity, gas, or water

To Learn More

Duden, Jane. *Floods! Rising, Raging Waters.* Environmental Disasters. Logan, Iowa: Perfection Learning, 1999.

Durham, Emma, and Mark Maslin. *Floods.* Restless Planet. Austin, Texas: Raintree Steck-Vaughn, 2000.

Gallagher, Jim. *The Johnstown Flood.* Great Disasters and Their Reforms. Philadelphia: Chelsea House, 2000.

Stein, Paul. *Floods of the Future.* The Library of Future Weather and Climate. New York: Rosen, 2001.

Thompson, Luke. *Floods.* Natural Disasters. New York: Children's Press, 2000.

→ Useful Addresses

Environmental Protection Agency
1200 Pennsylvania Avenue NW
Washington, DC 20460

Federal Emergency Management Association
500 C Street SW
Washington, DC 20472

Fisheries and Oceans Canada
200 Kent Street
Ottawa, ON K1A 0E6
Canada

National Center for Atmospheric Research
  Environmental and Societal Impacts Group
P.O. Box 3000
Boulder, CO 80307-3000

Internet Sites

FEMA for Kids
http://www.fema.gov/kids

**National Oceanic and Atmospheric
  Administration**
http://www.noaa.gov

National Weather Service
http://www.nws.noaa.gov

Newton's Apple—Floods
http://www.pbs.org/ktca/newtons/12/floods.html

Nova Online—Flood!
http://www.pbs.org/wgbh/nova/flood

U.S. Army Corps of Engineers
http://www.usace.army.mil

Index